Praise :

Ever wonder what ~~\~~ Flannery O'Connor had collaborated ~~u..~~ ~~\~~ result may have looked something (although nowhere close) to Jessie Janeshek's latest book...*Spanish Donkey/Pear of Anguish* is pure punch-poetry, it never misses a beat and it certainly never misses its mark. Read this book and be changed. Or better yet, read this book and change.
—James Diaz, *Anti-Heroin Chic*

The poems deliver verses on seductive female stars from the films of the 1930s and beyond. Like the stars they're watching, the poems become the empowered ones: language is theirs to play with, to betray....Each poem is impeccably crafted, syllable by syllable. The line breaks are as good as a crisp Pinot Grigio. No, wait, for the Bette and Lucy poems, pour yourself a martini. The Perpignan poems might like a tumbler of rosé."
—from the preface to *Invisible Mink* by Marilyn Kallet

This is what Janeshek does at her best—interweaves everyday life, the glamour and tragedy of old Hollywood, and our innermost fears and neuroses, which she bravely points out in herself so that we can identify.
—Shaindel Beers, *Contrary Magazine*

Invisible Mink is a book of empowerment. Syntactically risky and rigorous, Janeshek's narrators orbit around women—actresses of the great black-and-whites (indeed, Bette Davis makes the first appearance)—but also fictional characters of literary import such as Lucy Snowe, the protagonist of Charlotte Brontë's 1853 novel, *Villette*, who recurs several times within the book...*Invisible Mink* empowers—not only its author and the females on which it centers—but its readers, as well, as they come away with its energy refreshed and privy to a truly original voice.
—William Wright, *Town Creek Poetry*

Acknowledgments

"Hypersomnia," "This Church Is Celebrity," "How I Earn What I Owe," "We Come from This Hole," "We're an Attack Cat, a Blonde Tabby Troika," "Day Tripping, Geronimo Trail," "God's Gone, Mattress Soaked Through," "Call It Lead Woman Syndrome," "We Make a Pact," and "I Don't Know if I Want This" were published in the chapbook *Spanish Donkey/ Pear of Anguish* (Grey Book Press, 2016).

"Nostalgianica/The Bodyguard," "We Stare at Your Propped-up Corpse and Not the Camera," "Nostalgianica," "Nostalgianica #4: Break-up Season," "Bikini Selfies/Life Is Fleeting," and "Nostalgianica #3: The Home-Ec Parade" were published in the chapbook *Rah-Rah Nostalgia* (dancing girl press, 2016).

Poems from *The Shaky Phase*, occasionally in earlier versions, first appeared in these publications:

paper nautilus, Driftwood, Honey Pot Literary Miscellany, Luna Luna Lana Del Rey Anthology, Apeiron Review, wicked alice, Toad, Review Americana, Jet Fuel Review, Forklift, Ohio, Gargoyle, Milkfist, Bluestem, indefinite space, baldhip, Midwestern Gothic, THE DESTROYER, decomP, Pine Mountain Sand & Gravel, FLAPPERHOUSE, Literary Orphans Journal, Uut Poetry, Fruita Pulp, Rock & Sling, EXPOUND, Sidereal Journal, FRiGG, Pouch, Sonic Boom Poetry Journal, Broad!, Peach Mag, The Birds We Piled Loosely, Moonsick Magazine, Arsenic Lobster, Riding Light, and *Otoliths.*

The Shaky Phase

Also by Jessie Janeshek

Supernoir

Spanish Donkey/Pear of Anguish

Rah-Rah Nostalgia

Hardscape

Invisible Mink

Jessie Janeshek

The Shaky Phase

STALKING HORSE PRESS
SANTA FE, NEW MEXICO

The Shaky Phase

ISBN: 978-0-9984339-3-6
Library Of Congress Control Number: 2016961148

First paperback edition published by Stalking Horse Press, April 2017

www.stalkinghorsepress.com

Design by James Reich
Cover Image: Amy Davis in Jon Moritsugu's film *ModFuckExplosion*
Still photograph by James Dwyer, 1994

Stalking Horse Press
Santa Fe, New Mexico

Stalking Horse Press requests that authors designate a nonprofit, charitable, or humanitarian organization to receive a portion of revenue from the sales of each title. Jessie Janeshek has chosen Planned Parenthood.
www.plannedparenthood.org

Contents

Part One — 13

Part Two — 29

Part Five — 75

The Shaky Phase

Part One

Best in Show

I grow up wreathed
        in the Pontiac's highbeams
swallow drawbridges
        sink femurs in cedar.

You see me scream "boatglass"
        the sand trio chiming
my mood does not move
        from one man to the next.

You give blood at the chapel
        solidity convulsing
burn my sweet hairbow
        sprinkle its ash.

Abscess, adolescence
        I get my grasp back
creek rising, god willing
        angry and jealous
snowmelt surrounding
        my leopardskin dress.

Rural Legend

I'll leave this place
of motors, rust wristlets
once autumn comes on
and night cats eat the poultice
the lumberjack spread
to jaundice my heat.

The weight of your panic
is the way to my nurture
yet you say it's different
when we drink on the slagheap
preacherman lingers
and your infant son wishes
his legs away.

I knit shut my teeth
when it's all intake
dead batteries, cigarettes.
The stench of repairmen
is the stench of short days
cotton ball angels, mesh wings
and candlelight stretched
the wallpaper print in the attic
a mad kitten toile.

Lace oozes from eggs.
You tell me that grandpa
batted in twenty runs
left us death's secret.
It smelled just like whiskey.

I Wear the Tiny Blue Plates as Shoes

past the gut-splattered van   the sex edge over dust
   the wrench in my chest
pine boughs hanging.

It's not that I want
   the sirens to change me
   or need to be spanked
another day inlaid with rocks and red waste
the hoarse sluice of vanilla.

The small cat won't hurt us.
The smashed toad still moves
   pinning your hands to my back at the crossroad.

My natural state is black-stockinged
   one sunblade skinny and bald.
     I run hot water
swishing green sweat from the cactus
twist out of your mask and lead apron too late.

Baby America

He says every killer's a noir
    or a forest I paint wide-brushed
and some like to swallow
    alone on the first floor
    sore torture, my dust.

I wait for red thunder
    the crack of a pulled tooth
eyes on the snake cacti
    I wrapped in lace.

Stars shoot from her ears
    bassinette sticky.

I sweep the floor with his hair
    addicted to his hands
the broad back where I'd carve
    "Man of Constant Sorrow"

    kick the day open
    its blades unattainable
    and   God's onyx truth.
    rain on the cross in the grass.

This Starts with Girls Fighting Birds in the Foyer

I guess it's my strange way
    to let go the gristle
    bloat-smashed rubber roadkill
watch the dead opera   blunt love on the cusp
    through a bay window
   where fucking means nothing but time.

I guess there'll be glass
    once rain washes horseshit
and tusked pigs throw up on the pickups.

    Day three, where are we? Hooves and black pudding
drape the small body
    I try to taint.

This log house's lawn
    has its own genre.
Our trauma stretches
    across every ghost.

He Waited for Me
in My Infirmity Dream

Sore is the sad whistle
our treehouse turned inward

when you skin my hide
    light the watermelon candle

say *let's hear him bleat*
together sometime

when I draw claws on bricks
    miss his dark insides
the cold I called precision

I pop heart-shaped painpills
    abide my creation myths

            hooked in the old shack

                    fake chokechain tinkling

I'll Believe Prayers When I Suck the Dark Pipe

strawberry waders   addled with glass

that there's more to a chapel than lacing myself
    to this place in red sweatpants
my stomach domed.

                Where were you when the creekbed froze green
                and the men with machineguns
                drained each braised day?

It's quiet enough to hear the plant dying
    once I quit thinking
    start trusting knives

wait for white dogs
    to yank preacherman's sleigh
    kiss eggs from my brains.

A glittery cross hangs off each nipple.
In fireplace catacombs, Baby's bones sway.

How I Earn What I Owe

The clang stands for anger
    a low sun, a cat
                jaundiced and neon
green in its tail.

I sleep all day   next to my sidekick
watch the leaves' bead-gold diet
blue ants tracing cracks
wires, the stonewall.

                Your talking knife opens
                lank, hairy legs
                deerskull, triangle, and spine.

My hands are extensions
                what you do alone matters
of my fracture's haze.

                The hive drops a tomahawk
                snake, a blonde weal.

                We let the fox die
                rise like a birthday.

Bad for the Head but a Storm Could Remake Us

Ten necrophiliac deer
        dance on the creekbed
my spider-shaped fascinator
        gurgling with eggs.

I wrap myself
        in a plaid blanket
one shoulder unsavory
        feed the fire with your teepee.

Life dangles dark red
        soot coats your brain
and the thought of a desert
        will sterilize me
blessed, waxing tension.

        Everything's less
than the fox on the mantel
        your taste on my lips
blear and crystal.

Yes, the cage disappears
        when we paint your bones yellow
hang them from the clothesline.

This Church Is Celebrity

a vision of children
    in the log cabin
shot from my legs.
I'm declining your blindfold
    our father of syrup-stained
cotton, dark sex
      babyfat and a navel
shaped like a rhombus.

This absence is black-haired   a palpable habit.
    A priest wet with piss
    doesn't know if your broad back
      responds to my touch.

    I can't thatch your song
      circle the puddles
    the triptych   orange fleshed
      as time drains some crumbs.

Two Weeks and One Day

Time's playing hard tricks
a weird wall your syndrome
light blinking in as we sit cross-legged
shove the doll's feet
thinness and thieves on a pitchfork

Remember that summer?
    Spit and wing pain?
The redheaded me you could have shut
dark green gears, lamé?
The pull of sleep was not clean
and you hovered
    while I kept false safety
    behind the hutch.

    We play pathos, six ribs.
You run your claws in triangle shapes
knives western wide
sketch storms on my ankles
    warn me or warm me
men die at the end
before any moral.

We Make a Pact

a soggy gold box
a silver bee carcass

bleeding and cranky
drop to the duckpond

I straighten lost bones
in a wig and toboggan
push through your orange
weeds. Dayfright
stays with me as you fall.

You have a gun, cocked for the long haul
        automaton blonde.
The chapel-cast shadows blunt yet cutthroat
        I've nothing but thought.

Vodka Song / Volga Boatgirl

And don't you know yourself best
   when you're this close to death

all day lost in the loft smelling purple as sex.
   Japheth, vulpine, rad red Tantalus

offers you chocolate nails   horseshoes and cards
   a castle of claws   antlers that crackle

and nothing to drink   on the foam mattress
   but Pine Sol.   You knock it aside

call it a wash   sob for an hourglass.

Painstaking

You say the only good bird's a dead bird
when Sundays are empty
and most girls crave a witness.

I fill the oven with muscle
hope for a mermaid, a nursemaid
to spread the stovetops with slop.
I give myself leeway
to lean into bone
on the outskirt of meaning.

You shove my head in the lake.
I let the algae dry on my face.
They gawk from the swanboat
as you ride my dark part
the brain in the jar
the key to keep
then I crawl in the treehole
cheeping to bleed.

Part Two

The Best of My Love

There's a drip-drop of martyrdom
    to the hitchhiking kid
who climbed in your Buick
    begged me to hide
his blood-stained tire iron
made me want to fly shiny
    release a trapeze

    and whenever I bathe
that ragdoll that means us
she dries off hairy, smelling like hay.
    Her cry snags on green clouds
one more day   the creek's zenith
    my need to be held
        wild Christ on my knees
        my need for a scythe.

Some of our knives have been stolen, lost lids
    but I still fight the ghost cats
    lonely and angry to wit.
        So let me scratch this
        on the back of our death
        fill our night gloss
        with hobnails and latitudes.

Hypersomnia

I have it bad   big lumps   my head
    and, yes, I get caught
since if not guilt then what?
    And it's best to have something
a lover or clover   to pace the day dire
        to lick and contain.

What shape he makes
    in light's late convenience
as flies buzz my frizz
and pinpoints disperse
where the glass cat can't sex.

I'm dry and tapped
      over the land of our lack of tenderness.
      Organs withdraw
      chain wildwood nightmares.

      I live outside the deer
play the virgin   *which eye?*
play the victim   *which tear?*

I Don't Know if I Want This

    since all I do
is dig the red garden
    unearth the Sundays
I slept until sundown
    nuzzling a bottle of vodka
as you rode the blonde hollow
    legs spread on the tractor
inside a white dress
    wrapped the deer hides
in icicle lights
    wary of hunger
said summer'd be fine.

I fall right on your sweet baby needle
    cry when I bleed through your labcoat
onto nativity scenes.
    Everything's cigarettes, trouble and swish
        like the shell of the house
over the rockslide
    where the little boy fried himself
straddling car batteries.

    I lie back on the trundle
nursing your butter
    let dark Uncle Thick
tell me bumblebee secrets
and fleas bite my throat
    whet by your yellowblack rope.

Hydrotherapy

I wear my diamond-shaped
mask on the swanboat
narrow, bleached, beady
know I was born wrong
then you say the dream
where you beat me is progress
as I wade double danger
you say keeps us safe
baby patients screaming
bloody murder in the mud.

Then I take out the earplugs
to hear the path crackle
past the lake where daddy vanished
calves ripped by your beartraps
once wolves ate his gloves.

It's All the Blonde Turned Black's Fault

My lips shake with radium.
    My feet smell like stripes
wide sex, a trestle.
    I move through it all
in a clown costume
    turning glass purple
squeeze my bloody fist.

The sky stalls, glows brackish
    over the pigpen.
You lock yourself in
    know desperate mothers
    skin enemies best
and wrists need to rip
    for your prayer-drum to fit.

The Bible's rewritten in fluff
our bodies full of the lack.
    I write you *I was tired
of your whining not winter.
There's no logic in God*
    you say, seeing higher.
There's no logic in me
    since I can't.

All I Felt Was the Dark Boy
Manning the Swanboats

as I lay on the chifferobe
    waiting for vodka, three ambien

and you sawed the lawn yellow
    goosebumped and high
    atoned for the river
    gaped a silent film gesture
    my pussy's grape flavor
    wax-lipped.

Will you calibrate, initiate payback?
Can you roll the snake eyes against Japheth or listen?

The deer ran through the headlights, flatlining daddy.
He slammed my left leg in the door of the pick-up.

You Cannot Hear Me.
I Cannot Hear You.

It's spring and I'm past
the swings and our pact
trapped by the rockabye   house I attend to
the half-facéd cat.

Come to my bedroom, red phone.
I cannot trust
the planks or new light
awake to your threat
bit by bit. You say it takes
a certain white change
caught in the web of the hammock
to believe the warm notion of ghosts
and what's left of my heart's
a small furnace.

I'd like to say
I'm grateful for dissonance
coins and black wind
but this dialtone's a lie
and I'd die for transition.

Ode to Joy

It's disingenuous
to sleep through the day
when you're riding a lamb-headed
totem through fireworks
scratching morality plays in the dirt.

So I eat the mercury
hang from black rings
beg you to circle my ankles in duct tape
bludgeon the megrim from me
with a jumprobe.

> Whose hand slinks up
> the cat puppet's back
> mouths my desire's
> too greedy, taboo?

> Who shaves me bald as a child on the table
> spreads my legs in the loft
> satyrs my crotch full of sawdust
> as you jerk the ladder away?

It Gets to Where I Eat

nothing and drink whiskey.
    Japheth shreds the funny papers
    the big girl scrubs brown cups
    the puppy in the stockyard
    barking bitterness and fat.

It gets to where I ricochet
    between a triangle, an eyepatch
    and the milkmaid sorts the curses
    begs me to unpack.

Emzara will not mop, the barn's orange anatomy
soft as a Nerf ball.

It gets to if you loved me
    you would stage my loneliness
        throw me to the rain
let the grass concern   and the wasps' nest shriek.

You would hold my hair back
outside at the gravesite

where birds eat acetaminophen
    and there's no time like this present
red dogs on the fence.

God's Gone, Mattress Soaked Through

Obligations absolve the virgin
    shaped from the same cement as the birdbath.

Fuck me in thunder, but wives know the weather
    better than I
  and Zephyr won't leave the creek
before they find the brass skeleton
whiskered and kinked

    and this is my life, obsessed with catshit
my insides tingling.

    No food, no clothes.
I hear the white bear driving all night
    strapped to the truckbed.

Inside the whip of this lush world
    the devil sets down his pistol
the spider   a hacksaw   a red leather jacket
        to garden   (the storm passed)   horns clucking.

This Is the Shaky Phase

I make crises in my mouth
    harrowing the cat mask

lie down on the table
    jawing *contemplate.*

So you left him in the garden
      or maybe in a hot car.
    He could only come in rain
    jangling sharks' teeth in my face.

Tomorrow I'll leave hungry
    rummaging for arrows
    polka dot my toenails   red under duress.

The pink velour is nothing
      but a snakecharm
      or a smokescreen.

             Take the mask back off
             bat wings at the window flapping thick
             at the bright slam of the gate
             my shadow's chicken-shaped.

I Climb Down the Tree One-Handed and in Another Life

to varnish trains and paint a buck by number
my right eye twitching anthems
obsessed with melon braids.

Fucking left me empty
but I miss that icy month
handprints on my ass
pink stilettos under glass
and, afterwards, two capsules.

Third date I scaled the gate
slammed the Dodge into the slag heap
glowed in neon panties, my best paper bra.

The rain starts up again.
I scrub the wild dog yellow
name a concrete goddess
Our Mother of the Birdbath.

She says the world's no worse here
it's just I stay awake
half-cracked and waiting on the meat truck.

Part Three

I Don't Want for Reflection, Billy the Kid, a Duet for Five Fingers

Light's high through these bones
out of my sky and into your skull
as you said you could teach me
            each thump a descent
antler sequester   City of Rocks.

I can't tell if the barking's
woman or wolf
and cacti move slower than licking this evening.

You said you could make me a sentient being.
My vehicles do you no good.

I cry. I come sloppy
all over sundown
this tinsel nativity scene.

Day Tripping, Geronimo Trail

Deer trot along   my frontal lobe
  mill through black flecks   garbage and woodchips.

Deer gouge the girls   where winter limits
  and manmade lakes scald.

                The rain left the deputy
                possessing fake chimneys.
                We stripped, cripples' gifts
                dunes too hard to cross.

Why won't you release us
O spindly battery
O padlocked god?

                Left-brained girls left for dead
                on jack rabbit-fleeced beds
                we hitch our legs to fissured
                Rolando.

Holy Ghost Hook-ups
Sacred, Unafraid

I'm obsessed with dead dads
I hang them like prayer flags
   to ward off red babies
      who howl through my earth.

      Do you think I'm indigenous
         or disingenuous?
The rain leaves me naked.
I meet so much rain.

   I can't go to the mountain
to roll with the wolfkins
   in my dried flower headband
      and Peruvian clothes.
I can't ward off the man
   with non-Virginal cookies
who's probably casing the place.

But I know my vitals
   my shame, shame, shame
      keep away from black apples
         put on my pink hat
tell you I'm leaving
to work with the animals.

The Cosmology of America at Rico Valley Recovery Center

We ring around dead daddies
    of stardom and stagnation.
We ring around the blackthorn
    christened superstition.
We wring around our peglegs
    shatter Big Bang limbs
    the pregnant one ascending
cross-stitching fetal masses.

Sometimes I allow myself
pockets, God-thought screamy.
I'm still shiny in your dreamy
a blonde passion pumping gas
but it's draggy to be careful
in my silvering space capsule
cacti moving faster
than my crossings can recede.

See the Wolves!

I live your love on Kitchen Mountain.
          My presence means cages
          hung from wind tin.

Exhausted by arduous cryptozoology
          I need your Holly
          Hobby-hugged bible
          grit in my pussy
          white gesture of bone.

                              I had that bad dream
                              you knew my vitals
                              saddled my corpse
                              dumped it in sand.

                              You called me sissy
                              glass eyes in the firepit
                              sick mother duck ducking.

I'm one of those sites
along scenic byways
hatching the hounds.
It's all I can take
to stay in this town.

You Sell Me Geronimo

vinegar relish
    starving in dark clothes
fasten les masques
    to their black-rosed red faces.

In bed I leak pretense
    not sinking so much
deep throat beefy cake
    with a valence of one.

Performance art is too easy
    cursing first aid kits
as historic shards
    slash our violent estate.

To Cross Dunes in Boots Means
   Giving up

the glitter of history
   but my depths are guided

as I glide toward bullseyes

she winds the glass lasso

as I wear the shotgun
   his swung face a mess

Mesilla's old theatre
by the idylls of kingdom
come clothing, hi ho

memorizing your triggers
   like spurs or wildfire

around and around
the glimmerous cottonwoods

whine for Geronimo
of sandbag and hot slime.

We should be out

documenting the landscape

we should bloodlet
in canyon-sized hottubs
   say, intent doesn't matter
   when trapping's recessive.

Roadrunner, gnashed rabbit
   our shiny dice tragic
   we kneel at El Cortez.
   watch cotton-ball crèches ignite Silverado.

I'm Flouncing or Drowning
but Trying Not to Punish

I'm trying to belie
my fleecéd intensity
thought I'd be absolved
after cactus-based madrigals
and grease fires by now
but I still mix taxonomies
slink-binge in the sun
piss on the stick at White Sands.

You come in in all black
leg swollen thick
say fast growing plants
on dunes adapt psalms
the dog's name is Nugget
the snow smells like your pee.
Is my horse allowed
at the end of the monument?
You'd still have me
and all the Horchata you wanted.

The One They Shot, Past Your House

My Christmas present
My Christmas present
  gore when you fall
more tired than the first time

means stay in cages
means see the wolves
  you add matter of factly
  I fed them Composanto.

Bad means I walk
Bad means the nervous
Bad's in the antlers
  from blind clouds in the trees

Thin City to hurt
crank sugarfree
watching us fuck
  so you won't be lonely.

I'm sorry my kachinas
macerate spruce space
Desperada gussied up as Geronimo
Doña Ana knocked up   by a rattler and a stab.

The artificial lake changes my atmosphere.
It's the only way I can be narrator.

Infant Mortality. Compulsive Therapy.

I park my lamb and my sobs
at Lighthouse Church of God. Indigo's scanty.
Sights start to get interesting.
The man in the lot's doing hot-air push-ups
some cosmic relief.
I kissed his dog once (it was all bones)
threw my shoe against windows
in lieu of abortion
drop-kicked the RV's lumpy fridge like a liver.

I hate you today, done, pulled apart
    a sunchild assassin.
You wish I'd make time
    for your manmade lake
before the man in the van
    comes to get me?
I'm not your doctor but travel safe.
    Is this what you want me to say, sedentary?

The man with the cowskull
    says take water warm
this time of year. Don't bathe in the river.
    The winged cowboy leans
on aluminum cacti.
    I give up drinking
line my sequined pills
    start righting my idols
fall asleep draped on the heater.

You Need Me Your Ice, the Brightest in Town

I lack decorum
    a dirt road repurposed

I miss your wide moustache
    how you'd call me criminal
    slide in the hot springs ass first.

an ox cart or gypsum
    testosterone sun tricks.

orange tingle

The lake is ephemeral, albeit red-horned.
I hold the little green deer on blue dunes
wonder how much of this cold is psychology.

My hands will fall off
or I'll cut a hole in God's side to stay warm.

Part Four

The Pain of Young Want /
Blah Blah Blah Those Lost Days

It's trashy for me
under this tree
knocked up in black lambswool
a purple silk blanket.
As your sex tigerwhines
and your dick lionwinters
I hate you with raw snow
red meat, peace of mind.

I want to watch wolves
unearth vitamins
walk alongside
the delicate creek
but birds of a feather
phone-fuck together
and you didn't come
to this cross for a handshake.

I place my stethoscope on the moon
listen for bruises
until it's safe to expand
this hideous overhang
a protective resemblance
polarized and deployed
and my Soviet-era van
can withstand the thump
of your paramour's glistening tail.

Nostalgianica

Roll the ball on my hip
since it's time I contemplate
salmon polka-dot stalking
a white-slatted toy beaver
paddling your fragile
hand down my pants.

My silver tower
has an alternate title
I cannot remember
twinkle in heart shape.
It's where I score pain
weigh the needs of thrill seekers
against truth-seekers needs.

This is the space
I pray and thresh
the lemon dance costume
the pelvic ballet.
It's *where are we?*
and *may I sue for injury?*

Sending cellophane messages
seems the pale way to shred sense
but you need to know
you're in the midst
of a degraded experience.

Horses trot dry sheaves
and I already had plans
to go to the movies
but I'll stay home and hijack
your spinal fluid
your bell-clear cerulean phone

as we stab our backs
with static-filled syringes
naked save satin
Dress 'N Dazzle cloche hats.

I Used to Be Pleased

to curl in your motorcourt marrow
bike parked at the doorframe
exercise good   my tinsel transistors

instant absolution   orange Mary pain
but I left that party
just when you bit

my sex scent   silver panties
slurred on by red trade
and the late-height deer

or her wolf's-weight liquor saved.
I move raw all nights now
through fishflesh and whiplash

ice filling my sleep
fucking the eiderdown
out of my peace.

Time Seems the Chasm.
I Break the Glass

Can we even get back
    from cat piss on the floor
our ever-broad north
    a trick bridge over Taos?

    I've never been saturate
but what warmth when the plane
    pushes all your notes forward.

You went on a painting parade
    fake blood, gasoline
vacillate sideshow.
    You gave up the drink.

    I went through a long phase
of teenage gang debs
    sore throats   paper lashes
Styrofoam heads

want to go where there's no skin
    give ultimate oral
a cold Russian novel
    on the City of Rocks.

    You say no owl
has legs like that
    trust God's answer
creek crack   pipe shot.

You diagram
a certain dead hart
wrap yourself in the hide
        of its hind.

I want to find
        cedar squab houses pre-sunclose
be pulled through new towns
        on a leash of electrical sobs.

Hex Suck / Wolves Too

I wear the truce
two pairs of fur boots
talk in bebé voce
to my tarot card lay
hold *I'm the bad girl*
over the ice capades.
Swords say disgust
enough of this cruelty
but how much is sickness
how much is snow-move?

I skate this town hollow
almost a thawing
bowl spider dolls
welded from footballs
scrape at their furry antennae
and pray, rip Siberian meat
virgin boxes of beads
deer fat with the glass
poking through.

My wolves will not eat.
To dine on their den
is pine pain
a ring of black bells
or a sign of my worsening
character. Every minute I spend
enveloped in them
is a minute you lose.

Every Step's Ceramic

when typing makes me lonely
in the winter of red treadmill discontent.
My predilection's bladder burn
narcissism, chainsaws
walking Boston bridges.
I sing your sand psalms pregnant
in blue air bad for homeless women
bandaging choked rabbits
with stolen maxi pads.
I crack upon the lines
of my own symmetric crystal
and I just saw the paradox
in your red pores after sex.

I Thought This Was the Prank Call and My TV a Safe Place

so I masturbated
drew the short straw
watched Channel 8's long-term forecast.
Lockjaw, decimate
lumberjacks brewing beer
in my basement

> saying *I love you*
> *I was just thinking of you*

as I rubbed myself raw
with fabric softener

> spiders already filling
> up starshaped jars.

> I hate, hate, hate breaking news
> waking up in your bed
> panhandling correspondence

> > two hours of my life
> > donated to Bradley Cooper
> > I wait for snow and inevitable puke

> playing "Prelude Majestic"
> on a Yamaha keyboard
> in a pink clown wig, bodysuit.

The night rings laryngitis
my depression unheimlich.
I sit on a question mark
under your canopy

the pony dolls in blue pockets
next to the fridge.
My snowfall will damage
a car or small child

but there was that time
I put a note in your red mailbox
fed and pampered the cat
until it was happy
left to play villain
in a white sailor dress
my piss infected.

       I listened.
       It sounded like everything fixed.

Nostalgianica / The Bodyguard

May I sue for injury
　　some quasi-hope I can consume
　　　　when this song can't get past
the fleur-de-lis t-shirt
　　the cranberry chic jeans?

　　It's grim and it mystifies
the maxi-pad wedged up my ass.
　As I subdivide　　　　the abrupt
in a sustained exploration

I can't get past sixth grade's
　　　　cold bowling pins
　　when you leave me at the fête
　　　　in my Eva Joia sweatshirt
a VHS commercial　　　　your conjure corsage.

　　Is there some quasi-hope
I made a nudge toward great lit
　　in the underground shopping mall
　heavy with Nutella
　　　　　　　　and Lebanese pitas?

A leg lift a day　　　　　keeps the clear phone away
　　keeps me in fudge and wet cigarettes
　　and then they'll find Baby Spice
　　　　dead in her pearl dress
　shot by my squirt gun
　　under the sink at Hôtel Montreal.

What Does It Mean to Put This Away and Sustain?

I wanted to climb
    wander small pools
of black cacti blood
    at the City of Rocks
but the owl's heart-shaped face
    left no room for collapse
and I'm more languid than that.

I have you in my palms
    don't want your bone-toss
on the phone as our temperature drops
    and we list toward winter.

I'll strike my match
    on a blue Texas absence
    reusable gloves
wake to your grandfather's gritty obituary.
    You're not my polestar
and it's well past time
I start to work out my arms.

Nostalgianica #4: Break-up Season

I admire bravery
     clap on, slash the gauntlet
     my blood and food haunted.
I've fallen and I

cannot renaissance. Drinking white liquor
I ward the ghosts off
     keep choosing spindly
high femininity   lazy sex thresh.

     Plug in's the solution
a leg lift   a day trip
     the crux of it cold
on the kidneys, the ruddiest
          Eskimo cube.
I've fallen, and I can't

     Prince Strong Polyester.
     Bring me back dead ears
slick baby heads. I've fallen and I can't
     fake pregnancy cha-cha.

Your strength's in the ice storm
the piss intuition as old as sliced bread
     the drapery hook
you shoved in your voodoo doll's neck.

Nostalgianica #2: O Holy Nite, O Holy Nigh

It's penitential

measle epics blacken

this year of fast wings

glass eyes and chastity.

our skin of tinsel

the broken edge of January

Cats are addicted

snow with the sun out

blood behind mint

to water, dry skin

and you're the likeness

between hunter and hunted, like law

and I'm a new believer

in the great design

Virgin Mary

oligarchies

needlepoint pillows.

I wear places out

watch Muscovites die

go to heaven wrapped

in patched saddle blankets.

It's fenced now, fire containment.   I know the watch.

The meth-toothed fake angel

is dumping King Baby   straight in Cheat Lake

but if she felt   my pressure

she'd stop.

Nostalgianica #3: The Home-Ec Parade

I feel needy today
non-narrative, annotative, in love
with the skinny, vice principaled
oligarchy.

It's the penitent epic
an orange hand-sewn apron.
He asks me to name
the homecoming queen.

It's dark in these halls
the health teacher's balls burning off.
We've just discovered blow jobs and hairpins
our presence a used teddy bear.

Marcy's mother is pregnant
with triplets.
Her concrete mons pubis
mimics pornography
raw selfie structure.
These days we skip closure

so drunk we feed
off truth and hot oats
in Limited stirrup pants
and black bodysuits
can't leave the foodcourt.

We rebound, play dead
blue snow, sore throats
run back into school
with Christian dishcloths
for our choir director
that year of big boots
when it was so cold
our cats' bodies shut down.

Part Five

This Is Broad Humor.
The Weather Has Ruined You.

Hello, please sign in
give us purple blood.
I anticipate your hunger
my body a winter wonderland
our van heavy, fire-colored.

I ask how many Russians
does it take to xeriscape
freezing and cursing
this living history reenactment
and how many nieces
line this dark basement

when the existential walk on the glacier
isn't what it used to be
and Muscovites build
a snow maze for dog corpses
plan a second energy source
in that alternate language.

You leave to hunt
bear cubs on glass dunes
to pay back the love
your ankles circumscribing
my circumstantial
red ears and blue drugs.

Priced to Move

I slaughter all the houseplants
in my controversial panties

        jealous girls are pregnant
        know you love to bait me

I wear receiving blankets
fuck, fuck hairy pussy

        burning down the houseplants
        imagining Belize

I do light drugs all morning
feed and pamper breakups

        my flares subject to taxation
        unlocking daughter cells

I stagger to the foyer
we fuck in the corner

        I cheat on limitations
        our tight shadow has the heft

I shatter the transformers
let my body take the rap

        I think about going downstairs
        to grab my baseball bat

The Prince Is Cursed to Spend
Most of His Life as a Dog

It's a service that rewards
the failure of the service
   no time for headlight tonsils
   wet tinsel, dogged crosses.

It's a service that rewards

                    flat tire click bait haints.

   (Is your service existential?
   Is that why we sleep in snow?)

                    It's a service that rewards
                    the director with the horsehead
                    when atmosphere's a mess.

            We dream in flashback structure
            black and white yet red-lipped.
            The ghost looks like an apple
            a goalpost or a Soviet.

It's a service feeds addiction
when I'm just trying to live
            when the ice machine is broken
            in my 60s sidesplit
            and the dead skunk makes the driveway
            smell like sisters in a blender.

   I finish my dark liquor
   begin to think I love
   another woman on the video.

Bikini Selfies / Life Is Fleeting

In the spirit of the serpent
there's a baby breathes inside us.
We wear this dress: it's easy/dirty
pink eyes charging as we age.
We want rights to vulgar people
in non-vulgar seas. We want
the panorama: Niagara Falls-sized tonsils
and we want your prick to lead.

You'll say *what a beauty*, slide your mitts in
between our bumper thighs and funicular clits
and we'll thank you for your bald
and thoughtful statement
as our water medicates our foam ache and hate.
It's like the green cement casino
under Skylon Tower. It's like the guilt parade.

Experts blog our awesome navel
but our email is invalid and technology's a phase
so we wrap ourselves in Lelawala's doeskin
want the right to vulgar people
in this vulgar river. In the spirit
of the serpent, take this spade.
Does your prick die when we finish?
It's on the VHS tape, but we can't
lean on semiotics. Plastic panties
are no bother when you're just too tired to swim.

Note: The "Bikini Selfies/Life Is Fleeting" part of this poem's title was inspired by a
headline that appeared on my Facebook feed. It may have involved Kendall Jenner.

Broad Weather, for the Stars

It's time for plastic tokens
    slash, slash in this small town
our tinsel breath suspended
    above the liquor crosses
the toilets neon lit
    the most digital of guns.

It was only a fluke fluid
    amniotic piano leggings
    and we change our convictions
    pussies hairy in the moonlight
    your saddleburns reminders
    of just how much we love.

I always choose the purple
    enviable lipgloss
    two eggs in the hole.
    I always choke one twin
    and fuck the roofer
    moving toward a true sky
    of warm and special blood.

We're an Attack Cat,
a Blonde Tabby Troika

We buy in bulk   our mission accomplished.
We are a functioning individual

but we get tired of crying
inside our glasses

though paw-walking outside
let's us feel inspired
and fragmentation's our best citadel.

It was a gross mission. We got off
on the polka dot raft
teeth marks, inner tubes
the indoor theme park
progressive details.

We breathe too funny
red meat on spring green
our crimped hair so big
in that pink-toned cult picture
we cannot answer   the nursery phone

but get back to us   since Prince Stringheart says
he has a proposal.
The beef is a must   it helps our breath much

your hand sliding over
and out of our vulva
as we ride off on your black rocking horse.

Revenge Porn, Apathetic

Takes practice living this way
   naked in toboggans
blurry eyes sidewinding

     chest pains and psychopathy.
It's obvious we ask for it
   no talking to light history

compass pointy at a state shape
   sewage running down our faces.
We're horrible and we haunt

   unwilling to extend thought
to beings like ourselves
   don't want to give up hooves

armpits, dioramas
   his apnea and fat.
Every car that drives by

   says prosthetic scratch 'n' sniff
many minds will trust
   this, the coldest video

eat our foul breath in the dark.
   We were bleeding from the ceiling
dreaming of the ocean

   swording through black deer.
We were scared. We sang
   a free song. We lit our piss on fire.

Hark, Hark / Revenge Porn / A River!

Don't tell me days rise
when we stand behind, push
leave patriarchy
next to my tongue
the blue ice of our Flexible Flyer.

Red hair, Dairy Queen
don't let me believe
days won't go when I come
in your Dixie cup basement.

My heart mandate flickers
on your bearskin rug
the candle glow of your penis
my taxiderm dream.

I read Sausalito
cold masturbation
the Spanish girl's body
drowned in a water tank.

My ass fat, witch-print leggings
I insist you don't wipe up
my juice or the buffalo sauce.

Then we go door to door
barter moon candy
for darkly-carved UNICEF guns.

Slash, Slash O Siam

Seems like my star's rising
blonde head, greasy almanac
savvy when we both need
breast lumps, motifs.

> *Admit your addiction*
> *a snowsuit sucking blood*
> *from this hirsute circumstance.*

Today's when I'd rather
baste in pink naked
wait on black pain pills.
New babies, old babies
cost x-thousand dollars
frost slowly the sky.

> *For the love of Lady Lovely Locks*
> *who's going to cut you off*
> *pin you down?*

I'll feed and pamper
in February stock haunt
my sugar skull toggle
your wolf on the wall.

Like a bombed out cat embassy
a membership in misogyny
I'll keep ahead of weather
decide I don't care
when I see you or not.

This Is Broad Humor.
The Weather Has Ruined You Again.

I sit outside fuselage
in my seal chubby
smoking a pipe
Muscovites dying
of heathen pietas
or kidney disease.

Dance, dance propaganda
in loblolly garland.
Your hearth's just an image
of spiritual fishflesh
a pink indoor hottub
a sunken woodslide.

I use my fur
to put out your gold fire
ride my bike on the ice
make a joyful noise
when you shove in your finger.

We'd have one more day
In Crevecoeur, Missouri.
I'd bit off your
non-dominant hand
but here there's no time
for fetishization

a doll with words on it
stray moose in the yard.
I fall asleep in the snow
next to your crucifix
my Singer sewing machine.

Ghosts Confess with Purpose

The deer need their protein
                    so they eat the eaglet eggs
The spring clock wracks the trapdoor
                    so we unbubblewrap the floorboards.

I keep choosing spindly hexes
          Québécois-Scotch plexes
          cat puke catching flames
as the staircase curves like ice.

                  Cum-stained vases
          horse-drawn hearses, we're in mini-Europe
so don't let me off your hook. It predicts, and it appreciates
                as we maximize. So, let's talk hurt:

          I regret not scrubbing
          women puffing beads and mallow
       under three beef moons.

              What I mean is I was wicked
            when Eugene from Petrograd
               could not get hard on software
            and asked to see my tits.

We Stare at Your Propped-up Corpse and Not the Camera

We're a broadish yellow cult
handcrafted in bikinis

red Eva Joia sweatshirts.
We clean carry in foul weather

get our fevers on the lightbulb
lose all tit sensation

from imaginative sadness
and half-eaten Dairy Queen.

We sleep at the bear's den
to gain proof of his haunting

out of whack and watching
Peter Pan revenge porn

obsessed with Jean Naté.
We have too much Florida blood

to warm to lunar landscapes
suck pink glitter from his syringes

cream our panties crying fat.
Long sleeves are regression

on examination tables
as he links us to his ringtone

with skeleton damask
and we will or will not save

his shaggy head, our dying day.

Call It Lead Woman Syndrome

We turn on the hauntlight
    in this truth-seeking state
when every jumpsuit poem is purple
    and black cattle line the hottub
when sun-learned and flat-backed
    it's not our party.
Every rising seems exhausting.
    so we turn off our fight

    don't have time for cigarettes
or articulation. We don't ask for details.
    We're fertile. In spring.
We live in sore throats and dead trees
    insert the clear phones
under green sweatshirts
    Tinkerbell rub-on perfume.
It's been like this a few years
    snipe lights, neon stitches

our pink miscarried ache.
    Like victims. Impossible
spread across cul-de-sac dirt.
    We validate your subjectivity
strive to seem warm but not kittenish
    pull red poison yarns out of our nipples.
We still have one calf's
    white corpse in the basement.
Can you help us bury it?

Revenge Porn 17

We believe X-entities
unconsciously generate
poltergeist activity.

My prolificacy's your new friend
my axe your ethical dilemma
as our cats grow fat on absinthe
hog-weighting the blue chains

and we fight for snow prorated
hanging stars of David
inside our Potter Box.

It takes a few shush days
to forgive abominations
your heart the oily
target on my stump.

I toast the butcherbone
sleep across white forecasts
dreaming swollen boots and boobs
your crucifix, my nipples

too dark for the video.
We use our last fur coat
to clothe the human dartboard
smite the public's right to know.

We Come from This Hole

in standard blue unit
    to face the spring hit
    with the giant-sized teapot
    and pink processed cakes.

        Our head's at Palm Crosses
what's dark   what's enriched
        and we can't always swim
        the rubber-black myths
        without white baby cages.

        We want to get iconicity
        but handling sand
        makes our hands prickle
        and smell like a pigpen

                so we push toward liking
                since girls should be nice.
                So we say we're a wonderful creature

                choose to move past
                hot carpe diem
                when we want to show
                our seasoned teeth.

      Pain's just a sign.
      as we weep to the worm
      of our learned helplessness.
      The weather unexpectedly quits.

Spring Lag

It's a new era, baby
who will you marry?

Boston boots, dog bones,
or enchanted chincillas?

My prison wife fragmentation?
We drive to the beautiful

in gold bodysuits from the basement
hang gold body bags on the trees

but I'm too caught in the blue wool
they call calibration

keep thinking lime panties
mean limitation

the plastic Apollo
half-juiced on Thigh Beach.

It's a new era, baby.
Don't let me crowd it

with bullshit or spangles
as I shovel your fathers

in cold British theatres
where air is susceptible

and snow smells like piss.
We want to get theory

swallow horseblood
antlers and sprockets

so sharp they're scary
but we're much too guilty to stare.

Jessie Janeshek's chapbooks are *Spanish Donkey/Pear of Anguish* (Grey Book Press, 2016), *Rah-Rah Nostalgia* (dancing girl press, 2016), *Hardscape* (Reality Beach, forthcoming), and *Supernoir* (Grey Book Press, forthcoming). *Invisible Mink* (Iris Press, 2010) is her first full-length collection. She holds a Ph.D. from the University of Tennessee-Knoxville and an M.F.A. from Emerson College. She co-edited the literary anthology *Outscape: Writings on Fences and Frontiers* (KWG Press, 2008). You can read more at: www.jessiejaneshek.net

CPSIA information can be obtained
at www.ICGtesting.com
Printed in the USA
BVHW03s1141250918
528448BV00001B/34/P